T0143005

Abortion
The Debate

AGONY OF PERIODIC SPASMS

ROSS BRILLANTES
(GOODGRIEF75)

authorHOUSE®

AuthorHouse™
1663 Liberty Drive
Bloomington, IN 47403
www.authorhouse.com
Phone: 833-262-8899

Published by AuthorHouse   06/26/2021

ISBN: 978-1-6655-3054-5 (sc)
ISBN: 978-1-6655-3053-8 (e)

Print information available on the last page.

This book is printed on acid-free paper.

Part One

Preliminary and General Statement

Writing this book has been prompted, encited, encouraged by the intense discussion, elaboration, involvement of the general public on this matter of abortion. In decades past there has really been one dominant theme that controlled the global community: Against those who resort to abortion, against the medical professionals, the man-made severity for violation/transgression of the ban imposed by the overwhelming opinion.

This is an initial attempt of inquiry into the many sub-issues, ramifications, widening, deepening anger and bitterness on the main issue of abortion.

This makes an examination of the expansive meanings, definition, application of such words as "sin", "immoral", "killing", "murder", "fetus", "unborn child", "human being", "moral rights", "about defense" "the unprovable, unknowable God", "what the Holy Bible says", "after life", related words, applications both in terms of the human mundane world and in the realm of the spiritual, religious aspect.

Relatively new, somewhat iconoclastic terminology is being initiated here: "the union of the sperm and the egg cells".

From the perspective of the author most people in science, logic, and social philosophy are not conversant nor familiar with the postulate that 11 God is in control of "the brain cells, genes, DNA, and sensory organs;" collaterally with the sexuality of humans on whatever stage of their life.

As God is in control of the brain and all related functions, also included here is certain behavioral aberration of the LGBTQ community in relation to the mainstream society. Since God is God, He does things most humans would not comprehend or understand. Physical scientists are of the consensus they only 11 discover" - not maker/ creator of what God already made. The elements that hi- tech uses are God-made - long in existence but only lately discovered.

To better understand the logic of the narrative, it is fitting and appropriate word meanings and definitions are recalled for each situation under consideration.

1. Sin - A transgression of divine law. A deliberate or willful trespass of one of some religious or moral principle. Not man-made but God-made.

2. Morals/morality. adj. Pertaining to or concerned with right conduct or distinction between right and wrong. Capable of conforming to the rules of right conduct depending upon what is observed in human nature and actions or of things generally. Man-made as within each tribe, culture or society. God-instituted, God- created morals are in the

Holy Bible; the relations of man-to-man; man-to-God; and God to man. In particular in the 10 Commandments. To wit: "13. Thou shall not kill. . . 15. Thou shall not steal. . 16. Thou shall not bear false witness against thy neighbor; 17. Thou shall not covet thy neighbor's house ... nor anything of thy neighbor's.

Majority of Rabbis- as based in the Torah/Tanakh maintain "kill" misinterpreted as it should mean "murder". "Kill" is a moral right in defense of one's own life, the family's son, daughter, wife, neighbor; in defense of property rights, beliefs, principles, values. "Murder" is immoral, wrong as the killing is with malice, deliberate, based on anger, hate, revenge evil purpose, failed expectation.

3. Fetus I union of sperms and egg cells I embryo I fertilized female egg in the uterus I womb. It happens as a result of sexual acts of male and female. In biology, it is "It".

4. "Human being", "child" as explained by the Rabbis from the perspective of the Holy Bible / and / or Talmud, as it exits from the uterus and God must first "breathe life" into it in the form of soul / spirit. The spirit / soul is the "life" in the physical, mortal being. The spirit /soul integral part of God's plan to be held accountable to Him in the after life. Without soul /spirit, it is not yet human being. It is "It".

More common word meanings from American College Dictionary

5. Person - A human being whether a man or a woman or a child; a human being distinguished from an animal or a thing . . .

6. Abort - to miscarry.. the thing/ body fluid still in rudimentary state

7. Abortion - The expulsion of human fetus before - it - is viable - an immature and not viable birth product.

8. Fetus - Embryo. The young of an animal in the womb or in the egg. (Author: The union of the sperm and the egg in the womb or uterus of the Woman's body. No soul or spirit.)

9. Being - It means existence as opposed to non-existence.

The contents/text/narrative of this book can be misleading- not limited to, not focus on, not revolving on the title. Be that as it may- for the book title and the other matters and sub-issues are inter woven, interlocked into the center piece of conversation - convergence into the design, plan of the Creator, Maker, Synchronizer, Coordinator, the Be-All, and End-All of the entire human activity - in the earthly world unto the afterlife.

So move on to the elaborate discussion on God and theology; to the matter of science and religion; to the current controversies on morals on sexual drives; on LGBTQ; on gender identity; on the role of soul/ and or spirit.

The rather expanded coverage mainly influenced, dictated by the academic training, readings, study, experience, hobby-orientation of the author. He has to give honor and credit to his professors at Far Eastern University in Manila for his knowledge of liberal arts and science; to his mentors in the college of law at University of the East also in Manila; to Dr. Ronald R. Duterte (deceased} of the University of Southern Philippines, for engaging his service as college lecturer for six and a half years mentoring students in liberal arts and commerce (after his return from the U.S. after earning his 3rd college degree from the University of Houston).

Not to be set aside as part of his intellectual experience, he served for over six years as asst. city prosecutor of Cebu City, Philippines until retirement in 2007. Back to his family in Houston, he has been reading, studying, researching ancient cultural, political, social, religious history of the Holy Land and the general region to current times as part of active brainwork.

This being my 4th (and with prayer be the last one) writing work, I dedicate this to my brethren in Freemasonry –Lodge 1157 and lodge 1172 in Houston, Texas from knowing Ordinary Light to the Greatest Path of light known to mankind.

Ross ("Goodgrief 75") Brillantes.
Houston, Texas. USA, August 2019

As the author from infancy to adulthood raised within the umbrella of the RCC brand/ version of the Judeo - Christian persuasion, the aspect against abortion and related matters being presented - momentarily - on that perspective. From the past to current times the author has been immersed in the family, friends, the public-at-large of Roman Catholics; books, magazines, video and audio materials, scholastics upbringing in the same environment.

With that as the platform, the fiery dominant tirade against abortion in whatever form consist of the following:

a. -Murder of the defenseless child;
b. -Abortionists are murderers;
c. -The fetus is a live human being;
d. Medical doctors who perform the abortion work are for the money;
e. Medical clinics and/ or Planned Parent Hood facilities are in the business of killing babies;
f. There are over 65 million abortions.

AS general statement the life of living things must be protected; must be preserved; cannot be killed; cannot be hindered to full development; cannot be subject of medical and/or scientific study; cannot be subject of transaction.

Violation, transgression, obstruction, dealings, transactions about that "living thing", or thing or fetus or child or human is against the law of God, of humans. Subject to retribution, revenge, punishment both in the spiritual as in the physical, earthly realm.

As a general statement, any, some or all of the acts cited when performed is illegal, immoral, cruel, un-christian, evil, inhuman. That cannot be tolerated, ignored, disregarded or set aside or forgotten. As forceful- as candid in global scale - that must be globalized issue, matter. It is compelling, without shadow of a doubt being attended, must be addressed, minimized, suspended, eliminated from the earth. As faithful followers of RCC, this cancerous malady much be crushed without love, compassion, and mercy.

Part Two

God Manifestations

As made by commentator Goodgrief 75, many explosive power, invisible to the naked eye, comes from the unseen, invisible Being. Aside from the physicists of the atomic age, who would ever know the inconceivable force that comes out from the atoms of present-day nuclear weapons. Who could ever give power to the tiny brain cells of the humming birds from Mexico to travel to Alaska- thousands of miles away - just to suck in the nectar from tree barks? Who could ever give power to the tiny sensors in the eyes of the hawk to recognize a prey- almost invisible - while in motion a thousand feet high - to dive down. Well in fact, the vision tech of the drones came from nature as all others.

As shown in the NOVA program in PBS channel 8 in Houston, Texas, 11/23/2017, from 7 - 8 p.m., here are more super natural illustrations of the Almighty's power.

Japanese puffer fish makes six inches outer round figure and small round figure in the center, at the sea bottom, decorates it with eight lines end-to-end with almost perfect spacing in between to "entice, attract" the female as a process in mating.

Another of that super natural event shown is about the "resurrection" weed in Sahara desert. The weed completely dead for months up to over a year. Its tiny seed is bone dry under the searing heat. The desert wind blows the weed to some distant site. When the bone dry seed comes in contact with moisture or drop of water - the seed after seven days becomes "resurrected" into a new plant. That is power.

Before there is rational, sensible, logical discussion about morals, sin, killing, murder, exculpatory I defense I understanding of these complicated words and/or meanings, it is imperative the unseen, invisible God-spirit be recognized. The recognition that- although beyond the five senses of humans in the realm of the mundane, physical world- He has existence in the form of manifestations. For all body of knowledge - science, material, spiritual, religious, theoretical, logical - coordinated and synchronized - emanates from Him.

Since the age of scientific inquiry, it has been maintained and sustained that God is unknown, unknowable. But in current times - physical science has proved that compatibility, in accord, with the Scriptures/ Sacred Writings/ The Holy Bible.

Evidence There is a God - The First Cause and First Effect

The following writings/ books, authored by medical scientists can establish factual basis there is a God, a Creator, Maker, of the mammoth and the infinitesimal.

1. "Raising the Dead"- by Chauncey Crandall, famous cardiologist of Florida. The medical doctor has many personal, verified by staff, experiences of how by private prayer to the Lord God many patients, clinically dead - at one time or another- decedent by medical standard- resuscitated back to life and recovery.

2. "Back from Heaven"- by Dr. Mary C. Neal, orthopedic surgeon, ex-director of orthopedic surgery, who passed away for hours after being crushed by big boulders while kayaking in Chile with family.

3. "Proof of Heaven"- by Dr. Eben Alexander, neuroscientist, whose brain cells got infected by very rare bacteria, became brain dead, his soul I spirt went to the spiritual realm, encountered the invisible Who communicated by voice that the soul/ spirit needs to be back to the physical realm to continue the earthly work.

4. "Dying to Wake Up."- by Dr. Rajiv Parti, chief anesthesiologist at Bakersfield Hospital in California. White in the heavenly realm, his soul/ spirit was shown, given many f lash backs of his life of opulence, lack of empathy, desires for wealth accumulation, unattentive to the needs and well-being of others. His soul I spirit given the wisdom of humility, simplicity; after being united with

physical body, he gave up the lucrative practice into that of being a "consciousness healer".

Books may be accessed from Amazon or Christian Life Books.

———————————

Other works of Science that link with the Holy Scriptures consist of the following.

Sciences and Scriptures -Ariel A. Roth, Ph.D - Scientist, teacher and researcher (http://www.sciencesandscriptures.com/ScienceandScripture%Dr.ArielARoth)

"Dr. Roth has been active in the evolution- creation controversy ... He served as consultant, keynote speaker, or witness for the States of California, Oregon and Arkansas. He spent 30 years of research work. His book 11 Science Discovers God11 is at the Adventist Book Center.

Among many things his book "Origins: Linking Science and Scripture presents scientific evidence that authenticates the Bible has been published in 17 languages. Key issues related to the "God Question are as follow:

* The intricate organization of matter in the universe;
* The precision of forces in physics;
* The complexity of the eye and the brain;
* The elaborate genetic code;
* The disparity between the fossil record and the vast amount of time necessary for evolution.

More science: "Origin by Design"- rev. ed .. by Robert H. Brown, Harold C. Coffin, L. James Gibson all Ph.Ds. . Also in Adventist Book Center. "Understanding Creation" by Dr. Humberto Rasi.

Sheets

Since God is a spirit, a ghost, a thin cloud, or a faint white shadow, generally He is not visible to the naked eye. It can be stated He is like oxygen in the air that gives life to living things, unseen and invisible. In fact His existence is not subject to the four senses of sight, touch, smell, and taste. Although He is supposed to be unknowable, He is known, He can be seen by way of His various forms of manifestation. Generally that manifestation is a product or a by-product -not an unfinished work or task.

Evidence, proof that He is the First Cause, Maker, Creator, Synchronizer, Recycler, Originator of the origin; that He indeed exists. In effect this validates the assertion that nothing come from nothing". In another way of saying, "something comes into being because of something ...

Here are a few scientists in the field of physics, biology, zoology, geology who spent over 20 years of their skills investigating the god-origin. Dr. Ariel A. Roth, published his Book of Origins: Linking Science and Scripture which presents scientific evidence that authenticates the Bible- in 17 languages. His new book titled: Science discovers God:

Seven Convincing Lines of Evidence for His existence. Available in Adventist Book Center.

Continue: Origin By Design, revised ed., by Robert H. Brown, Harold C. Coffin, L. James Gibson; with Ph.D in Geoscience; Ph.D in physics; Ph.D. in biology, respectively. Also in Adventist Book Center.

Dr. Roth examines key issues related to the God question... namely: The intricate organization of matter in universe; The precision of the forces in physics; The complexity of the eye and the brain; The elaborate genetic code; the disparity between the fossil record and the vast amount of time necessary for evolution; among others. (For the curious about supernatural contact Sid Roth at Daystar TV network in Dallas, Texas who spent over 30 years of study, observation, and monitoring.)

In the 1980s, the RCC entities have blanket control on any form of abortion, the severity of worldly and spiritual penalty, psychological, and mental penalty. Well funded, well connected, well supported by apologists entities consist of: American Needs Fatima of Pennsylvania: EWTN of Alabama: National Shrine of the Lady of the Snows, Missouri-- Missions of the Holy Trinity, Maryland Association of Marian Helpers, Mass- the archdioceses that encompass the whole USA.

The resources of the entities are endless, without bounds, without obstacles, cannot even be hindered by the unseen, invisible divine, the Eye in the Sky. They are in control both in the physical, material realm as in the spiritual realm.

How do the Pro-Life, Anti Abortion zealots indoctrinate, prosyletize the global community with their rigid, dogmatic teachings that make governments make laws so severe in their favor? Through their global community of fund raisers. On each minute, on each hour, millions and millions of people are inundated with offers, solicitations, masses, intercessions, healings from thousands of religious orders, societies, affiliates- with a "little" gift, donation, contribution, here, there, and every where.

From the poison, toxic teachings, messages, slogans, hell fire consequences poured from all directions by the entities, this world becomes polluted, contaminated with hate, disgust, despise, warfare. No longer with ideas but feelings of retribution, revenge, vicious incarceration.

The PUNISHERS on abortion make the prohibition as the punishment aspects so severe that shot gun the message for total ban on that medical procedure. In effect that is total brutality, without kindness, love, compassion and mercy. Shade of the inquisition which ruled for 500 years; of the Spanish Conquista for over 300 years of the "Christianization 11 for 340 years in tandem with the 1st, 2nd, 3rd Crusades and the Cathars Crusade when millions perished.

This is the foundation of moral, religious, biblical, God-sourced teachings. Not by priests, nuns, religious orders, or societies; not by pastors, ministers, nor human mediums used in 360 apparitions, appearances of the impostor Virgin Mary (not the Jewish mother of the Jewish Son nor descendant of the family tree of Jewish Jesse).

"Thou shall not kill" - through the centuries has been and is always understood in the literal sense. Kill is kill. It means killing that results to death. Death of a living being. As the 'Raid' insecticide product claims, it kills the bugs dead!

This commandment was, had been and is being addressed to live, human beings. It is addressed to humans at the adult stage, at the age of discernment; the capacity, capability in distinguishing what is right and what is wrong, what is good and what is evil. For the totally insane, totally deranged, without free will or voluntary choice, this commandment is meaningless. Evidently, this is not applicable to infants, small children.

Ross Brillantes

Now this literal application - is it the right, correct, inflexible, rational, inevitable meaning in all situations. Luckily it is not. Certain Messianic Rabbis in the Daystar TV network in Dallas, Texas recently- June 2019, disputed that line of thinking. In the Moses Law, "kill" actually refers to murder which has an entirely different meaning, application.

"Killing" per se is not immoral, not evil, not wrong. It is even a human right. Killing another person in defense of one's life, for his son, daughter, wife, family member is a right to life. It is also a right in the process of "hot pursuit" against the offender who initiated acts of killing the victim. Defense of property, belief, value, from severe provocation (s) can also be an exercise of that right.

The quality, character of "killing" changes when it is tantamount to murder". What is murder. When the killing is done with malice, evil purpose, hot under duress or irresistible force but performs the acts of execution.

The beginnings of human life

As nothing comes about from nothing/vacuum/empty/ void – it is inevitable there is a cause that results to an effect. That cause that produces the effect is the unseen, invisible God-spirit. That invisible spirit came to the knowledge of humans through the Holy Bible. He is all powerful, omnipotent, omnipresent. He is creator, maker, Synchronizer, master Coordinator.

He created Adam from clay and breathe His spirit in creating the adult male. In His wisdom He took one left rib from Adam as the male needs company from the misery of loneliness and boredom. Again he breathe the spirit in converting the rib into adult female. Thus human life came about as adults. Not as fetus, not as sperm and egg cell. His breathe in the form of spirit gives the life.

Before Adam and Eve He already created His messenger called angels. Angels are spirit with God-like powers, but when one third of them rebelled against God because of pride, ambition, jealousy, they were cast down to earth to become demons. One of them turned into a serpent that tempted/enticed/cajoled Adam and Eve in eating the fruit of knowledge which consists of bad and good, evil and godly, right and wrong.

In the countless generations that follow, as God is God, He created the sperms in the male and egg cells in the female the union of which shall become the likes of Abraham and Sara in perpetuating the human race honoring, adoring, praising Him and obedience to His ordinances.

When that union becomes fully grown into human form capable of exiting the uterus/womb… He gives the breath of soul/spirit that stays with that physical being which sustain its entire life time. Proof of that soul/spirit becomes identifiable when the brain cells start storing memories/images/recollection after the age of two years. That's the consensus of brain scientists/neuro scientists. (Note: manifestation of soul/spirit is the death of the physical body and its exit into the afterlife as given in the personal testimony of many medical doctors and professionals in the state of NDEs.

How about those in acts of God? when He decimated the Egyptian people with plagues and death of the first born male child? And those warriors chasing their intended victims who drowned in the middle of Red Sea? God was defending the lives of His Chosen people. No malice or evil purpose - but for a noble, laudable deed.

How about those soldiers/ warriors in the war zones, in times of mortal combat. They are engaged in killing soldiers/ warriors of the opposite army. They are performing a duty, following orders, in compliance with their chosen career or profession or means of livelihood. Now this is a grey area that cannot be addressed in general, sweeping terms. That is better left to the judgment of the Mighty High. For He alone holds the evaluation, judgment on the soul/ spirit of each dead body; He alone based on the life history of each individual can render kindness, compassion, forgiveness or eternal damnation.

Religious/ Human Anger on Abortion

This is year 2019 - and the anger, hatred, vicious tirades, condemnation against abortion / abortionist has been going on for decades. The initiators, the concerted global forces versus this issue/ matter have been from the RCC, its institutions, its agents. From their worldwide constant, regular, incessant multiple methods of barrage on the issue, the global community has become indoctrinated, inculcated to their agenda.

At this period in time, the power, prestige, dominance, control - as it has been for centuries -on the agenda lay in the hands of the most numerous church. For one, it has over 400,000 priests, thousands of nuns, millions of adherents who - on daily basis bombard the world community with their agenda. Is that agenda the truth, the whole truth but nothing but the truth on rational, biblical basis?

Going back to the scenario at the Garden of Eden. God could have taken out the free will, the free choice of Adam and. Eve... He could even killed them and replace with another set of humans.

Hebrew Jews
The Holy Bible

Generally, among Christians the biblical story about the Jewish son of the Jewish parents being recognized and accepted as divine, borne out of the Holy Spirit. This Holy Spirit is one of the countless manifestations of Yahweh, the God of Israel, of Patriarch Abraham.

The Jewish descendant named Merriam/Mary, descendant of the Jewish family tree of Jesse, also descended from distant generations to the Israelite King David's tribe. This Mary is to bear the Son of the Holy Spirit as spoken to the prophet Ezekiel 500 years before Jesus becomes the divine in human form and flesh and 200 years earlier by the prophet Isaiah

Although claimed as virgin then unto forever, the wife of Jewish Joseph had a son James in the marriage. Being in the state of marriage, by any rational, logical, thinking, it is simply impossible Mary remaining a virgin from start to finish. By virgin by any meaning means, the hymen never externally penetrated and broken, no sexual relations took place between husband and wife. That is total absurdity but billions just say

"Amen" without objection, without question - particularly those in the religious profession.

Now this Jesus is both God-made and man-made. The holy spirit supplied the invisible sperm, and Merriam provided the egg cell in- waiting in forming the future Redeemer, Savior, Messiah to the Chosen People and to the Gentiles.

Now that is the first supernatural in the so-called New Covenant. The real one, not fake.

But the millions who are die hard against abortion would not even allow women to exercise their free will- their free choice in electing abortion as the last resort for each particular situation. Each person experiences spasms, bleeding, recurring pains, enduring discomforts, ongoing anxiety on how to provide decent, continuing support at later times when unform child becomes a human being in the outside world.

The extremists to abortion and to its medical procedure surround themselves with dubious morality, unbiblical belief, unscientific abracadabra, wild imagination, sadistic ideas.

The real, actual, impending threats women in exercise their free will, free choice to abortion is immoral per see because God gave them that right. What God gave to humans, only God can forbid.

God gives all humans the right to life, to liberty, and pursuit of individual happiness. Each individual woman – in her particular situation – has the right to pursue, enjoy her own way of life as her conscience tells her so. In religious, theological, spiritual sense, the Holy Spirit is the person's conscience. What is the consequence/happens when the person's conscience/holy spirit violates the Creator's ordinance. Humans cannot arrogate/install into themselves severe imprisonment on women's right to abortion.

Only God can sanction that spirit/soul when it departs from the physical, mortal, body. He and/or the angels do the processing as to what kind of life the deceased was pursuing while still on mundane earth.

Part Three

Just Supernatural

The coming of the holy bible into the Holy Land of Israel, its 66 books of the Torah/Tanakh and the Apostolic Bible together is in itself a super natural way of disclosing the super natural. The Being of Light initiated or provided the clue to His existence. Before the Scriptures, planet earth was inhabited humans without regular, daily ordinances to follow except on their own fellow human beings. Mainly humans existed purely for survival and procreation.

As given by Himself, He initiated relations with the tribe of Noah. By voice, He communicated initial ordinance of love - that humans live together in harmony, cooperation. Help, assistance as community for continuous survival of the race. But the demons carried on their evil designs upon humanity. So to provide a clue to His creatures as to His presence, He communicated the warning of a great flood; that for them to prepare according to His instruction. So it came to pass, the f lood came and ended – the human race continued to exist.

From the roots of Noah's tribe came the house of Abraham. From the seeds of Abraham, came the Hebrews. From them the Holy Bible as the fruit of the labors of the prophets. That holy book becomes cultural, religious confirmation of His Being.

Omitted by intention and design is any mention or reference why- why oh why- women have abortion/miscarriage. EWTN and RCC tv networks are so angered, bitter to the medical procedure. No God-like redeeming act/gesture of kindness, compassion, love, forgiveness. {It is the usual 11Christian" version of satan.}

The over powering, dominant, over whelming forces against women's exercise of free will, free choice have not taken the time, effort, study, research as to the basis, validity- both in the realm of the mundane and the spiritual - of their concepts of sin, kill, morality, vengeance, fetus, circumstances of their preys under relentless attack.

Recently one -of many new predators on abortion arrived in the household. It dangles itself as "And Then There Were None" said to be founded by Abby Johnson. She claims as former Planned Parenthood clinic director. "For eight years I worked to the abortion industry.... I started as a volunteer for Planned Parenthood in College Station, Texas and over the years worked my way up to Clinic Director".

The goal/purpose of her movement is to ask people to provide a "lifeline" to quitters from the abortion industry, particularly those working for abortion providers. With no more professionals/staff workers in the "abortion" industry, abortion comes to "complete eradication". In fine, she is soliciting through her organization - sustainable funds for ending abortion and provide support to quitters from the Planned Parenthood.

Another potential entity for tax deduction and tax exemption. Being covered up/ masqueraded as "means of good intention using the path of vengeance and revenge" using the lawmakers and police enforcement.

———

Reactions/ Comments on LGBTQ
Source: Yahoo - Entertainment I Raechal Shoefelt- ET Editor July 31, 2019

———

"Mario Lopez apologizes for ignorant and insensitive comments ...

"The comments I made are ignorant and insensitive and I now have a deeper understanding of how hurtful they were," Lopez said in a statement to Yahoo Entertainment, "I have been and always will be an ardent supporter of the LGBTQ community and I am going to use this opportunity to educate myself." Moving forward I will be more informed and thoughtful.

The same source for the following.

Goodgrief 75

"Thanks for Mr. ET Mario Lopez for being an ardent supporter of the LGBTQ community. You are part of the small, minority of supporters. Always be strong- you have the support of behavioral scientists in the Kinsey Reports- 1948 and 1953. Access in the Wikipedia. Moreover, you have support from the biblical God Who controls the brain cells, genes, DNA, sensory organs of humans. Hooray to Mr. ET!"

The global punishers/advocates/initiators most represent the teachings/slogans/ of the RCC. The clergy, nuns, believers of this institution for centuries have been engaged in deception, omissions, masquerades, bold lies to make their agenda credible, sweet tasting, easy in swallowing. Their accusations, intended consequences for the abortionists/ miscarriages:

1. The woman – millions of them – are likers/ murderers for both miscarriages and criminal abortion. No factual, real, documented evidence of the 65 million. This is deception;

2. The women who exercise their free will, free choice – whatever their situations/circumstances of spasms, recurring pains, repeat discomforts, anxiety of future decent support for another human – are killers/murderers as the medical doctors consigned tom imprisonment for breaking the laws of U.S. lawmakers. This is speculative lie because most violators are not caught and prosecuted.

3. Expulsion of the union of the sperms and eggcells in the womb could not be conjectured/speculated

as killing/murder for reasons of: The adult woman is exercising her God-given right of free will, free choice – answerable to Him; the sperms and cells are not humans; embryos in animals have heartbeats

4. The RCC apologists have bitterness in their minds and heart – they lie.

"Jews, outraged by restrive abortion laws, are invoking the Hebrew Bible in the debate

"It's common in this debate to hear the Christian perspective. But what's often left out ... is how Jews, who read the Hebrew Bible (the 1st, original, as founding of Judaism, 3,500 years ago - author) ... that their tradition condones abortion. Sometimes, when the mother's life is at stake -it even insists on it (abortion).

"This is big deal for us", Ruttenber said, "We are very clear about the woman's right to choose. And we are very clear about the separation between church and the state".

"Within the Jewish tradition' tikkun olam '-Hebrew for repair the world- is sort of a call to action- a concept of a call to kindness and service to heal the world. . .. For rep. Wasserman Schult, the first Jewish woman elected in Florida, her faith informs her politics every day.

"As for me, when I'm thinking of the woman's right to make/ her own choices, the Jewish tradition that I have always been taught holds that existing life should take precedence over potential life, and a woman's 'life and her pains' - should take precedence over a fetus."

"The strongest argument in the Hebrew Bible for permitting abortion comes from Exodus chapter 21 verses 22-23: If people are fighting and hit a pregnant woman and she gives birth prematurely (miscarriage) but there is no serious injury, the offender must be fined whatever the husband demands and the court allows.

"In this passage gives 'birth prematurely' means the woman miscarries, and the fetus dies. Because ... the person who causes the miscarriage is not liable for murder. Jewish scholars argue this proves the fetus is not considered a separate person or soul.

"The Talmud explains that the first 40 days of pregnancy, the fetus is considered I mere f luid' and considered part of the mother until birth,"

Source: Yahoo G. Todd Garrin 6/4/ 2019

Sunny Hostin slams Catholic bishop's anti-LGBTQ stance:
I know Jesus ...912 reactions - top reactions

Goodgrief 75

To critics of LGBTQ, particular Roman Catholics: You
need upbringing knowledge about the unseen, invisible God
out of the RCC version. He exercises His awesome power
of modifying, changing admixture of the genes, brain cells,
DNA of men and women, such that males have characters,
elements of females and vice versa. Already confirmed in
the Kinsey Reports (1948) on human sexual behavior, by
Alfred Kinsey, Paul Gebhard, Wardell Pomeroy, Clyde
Martin (1953). Research on Sex, Gender and Reproduction
founded by Albert Kinsey of the Kinsey Institute at Indiana
University.

Main excerpts: 11 Kinsey avoided using the terms like
homosexual or heterosexual to describe individuals,
asserting that sexually is 'prone to change over time and that

sexual behavior . . . both understood as physical as well as purely psychological phenomena (desire, sexual attraction, fantasy). Instead of three categories (heterosexual, bisexual, and homosexual, Kinsey used the seven point scale system... "A person who identifies bisexual for example may sexually prefer one sex over the other. Sexual preference may also suggest a degree of voluntary choice whereas the Scientific Consensus is that sexual orientation is Not a Choice" (This proves God's modifying power!!!).

Here are real, factual, well-documented stories about the irresistible power of sex drives.

Source: Yahoo News Dec. 28, 2017 (social media) Mythill Sampathkumar, The Independent

"Father 'found 13-years-old son and 44 year-old teacher for having sex in car'

"A father has said he found his teenage son having sex in the back of the car with a teacher from his Texas school.

"Police in Bay City, 80 miles south-west of Houston, have charged the teacher, Rachel Gonzales, 44 with online solicitation and having an improper relationship prior to the alleged incident on 14 December, police said.

'At the request of the District Attorney, the Bay City Independent School District, where Ms. Gonzales is a teacher, have turned over the case to the local police...."

Source: Yahoo News March 27, 2018 US NEW Your Post

'Woman in romantic' relationship with brother charged after giving birth; cops

"A Florida woman, reportedly in a 'romantic' sexual relationship' with her brother was charged after giving birth to his baby, officials said. Pauline Elizabeth martin, 33, told investigators she and her brother were living as a couple in Groveland when she became pregnant with his child, the Orlando sentinel reported.

"Authorities said they began investigating the woman, who is a cashier at McDonald's after the baby was born Nov. 21, "with severe medical problems". The newborn was immediately transferred to get specialized care at Winnie Palmer Hospital for children in Orlando, where genetic testing revealed the parents were related, the Daily Commercial reported. Neither parents completed…."

These are many manifestations of God's power and control over the brain cells, genes, DNA, sensory organs of humans.

The Supreme Architect of the Universe is really behind this narrative. That's why just every human behavior {not infant, not new born child) is not included in this book. It is to be noted again that neuro scientist / neurologists/brain specialists generally concur the young child/infant cannot store memory before the age of two. Memory storage begins to develop after age 2- which is a manifestation that God has given the infant His breathe of life in the form of spirit I soul.

"Former Christian school teacher, 29, arrested days after being caught in bed with teen boy by husband: cops

"A former Oregon school teacher was arrested after being accused of having an affair with a 15-year-old student that lasted for more than a year, authorities said Monday'. Andrea Nicole Baber, 29, was arrested at her home in Cottage Grove last Friday, the Register=Guard reported. The arrest . . . came days after Baber's husband allegedly walked in on her and the teen in bed., according to the News-Review.

"The student's father reported the relationship to police Dec. 12 after he and his wife received an anonymous email asking if they knew the boy and the Logos Christian Academy teacher were in a sexual relationship, authorities said. The message was attached with photos of the teacher and the boy."

This supports the general perception of physiologists that the female genetalia has more sensitive nerve endings than the male. Thus when the sex act tried a few times the desire gains momentum.

Part Four

Application of Morals/Morality

Millions - in particular in the three major religions - Christianity, Islam, Judeo-Christian - use moral / morality values on a one-way perspective. What their particular agenda at a period of time, place, culture, environment - would be, regardless of the wounds, hurts inflicted on others.

What is one- way moral value is this: What is self-fulfilling, self-gratifying, self-service to the ego of the initiators, to the proponents, to the punishers.

The morality is to prevent the exercise of Free Will, Free Choice; if not complied by the non-conformist, disobedient, opposing morality, then use criminal law in its ugly, oppressive, sever imposition upon the adversary.

There are many views to morals/ morality both on the mundane and spiritual, in theory, in practice, in non-observance.

Morality has always been used as a means to oppression, cruelty, evil ends. The reality of wrong, bad, evil, is almost always disguised/ masgueraded/ deceitful - generally good-looking, palatable, appealing, beautiful.

———————————

Underneath/ behind the good looks/ disguise are indications of Lack of empathy; lack of kindness; lack of compassion; lack of mercy - on the stronger side: enduring anger, spite, bitterness.

On the God-like, humane-like side of morals, gentle, pleasant indications consist of: Compassion to human weakness, frailty is a quality of morals; respect to the exercise of Free Will, Free Choice is a quality of morals; honoring God's gift of free will, free choice, His final judgment in the spiritual realm of the after-life is powerful and divine morality.

This discussion is not closing nor ending the debate on abortion. For on the side of the RCC teachings - many of them - they are on the side of the infallible, the devil's version. For every failure/ error/ evil, three is a reason, for every reason, there is an excuse, for every excuse, there is a reason - round and round in circle.

What is the "After life"? The relevance to abortion issue?

It is related, connected, when the physical, mortal human body dies as an NDE or when it dies completely without the spirit/soul coming back to restore what is known as "human life". Either way the soul/spirit is relevant for God's purposes.

Extensive account/narrative can be found from hundreds of NDEs (Near death experiences). Such NDE experiences recoded, compiled in the book: God and the After Life with sub-title: The ground breaking new evidence of God and near death experiences. The authors: Dr. Jeffrey Long, M.D., New York Times bestseller of Evidence of the After Life and Paul Perry.

(Harper One - An imprint of Harper Collins publishers.)

———

Here is a brief, condensed in a nutshell, the afterlife journey of Dr. Rajiv Parti, M.D. "He described his soul's journey at the edge of heaven and hell. While at edge of hell he heard voices of cries, moans, anguish below. AS the spirit kept floating forward, there was a continuous flashback of the melancholy, unpleasant side of his earthly life, unfolding before his eyes.

As the soul was transported to the bright but not blinding light, it was a place of absolute peace, with green grass and plants, vibrant f lowers with no earthly existence. The voice communicating with the soul gave message about goodness, kindness, soft-heartedness, empathy to fellow humans. That message was new wisdom implanted into the spirit. The worldly joys, fortunes of wealth, lack of empathy not worth of lasting happiness. After that spiritual journey, the medical doctor gave up his lucrative practice as chief anesthesiologist. He settled down to helping people in pain and suffering, and has been practicing" Consciousness Healing "in California".

Part Five

Why the Devil's version of morality prevails
And why the Morality of Abraham's God would sink

After emperor Theodosius of the Roman Empire by decree in 380 A.D. created the Holy Roman Catholic and Apostolate Religion, man-made morality became more violent, rigid, wide spread in the so-called Old World and beyond.

That violence, rigidity of man-made morality became the immediate cause of torture, death to millions under the over 500 years of the Inquisition, in concurrence with the 1st, 2nd, 3rd Crusades, Cathar Crusade, Spanish Conquesta in global scale for 340 years. (Circa 1211 to 1825.) All mass, organized violence in whatever form against the heretics, pagans, Jews, Muslims infidels under the umbrella of the interlocked, interwoven fabric of church and the state constituted violence against the teachings of love, kindness, mercy, forgiveness of the invisible, divine God of the heavens.

Voice attacks, digital attacks, print attacks, prison terms visiting upon miscarriage, abortion, in the exercise of God-given free will, free choice, as globally carried on by RCC and its rigid believers form integral part of the man-made morality.

That is why resistance to the man-made morality - even how disadvantaged, how little impact, how less effective against overwhelming number, must persist.

Years after the Roe v. Wade law to current times being year 2021, the momentum in global scale is in favor of the devil. And why not? Satan/Belzeebub agenda has been succeeding for too many centuries.

Undisputed illustration being the relegation of the religion and the church of Jesus Christ, His apostles, as the prophets of ancient times from mainstream religion and its history. For over a thousand years the Jewish cultural religion of Judaism, the place of religious worship called Tabernacle/Synagogue-church - have all disappeared in the global narrative.

The Gospel of Good News - had and continues to be used by the devil to glorify successes in empire-building, wealth accumulation works, spreading lies, omissions, deceptions in indoctrinating the human race of its own version of agenda.

In more particular, specific endeavors, the devil vigorously pursues Pro-Life, anti-abortion agenda concealing the evil desires in imposing prison terms, economic hardships, legal impediments to the God-given rights of free will, free choice.

By deceptive device it pretends being advocate of "thou shall not kill" as written in stone to Hebrew Moses. That ordinance is addressed to human beings with discernment - never to those in the uterus.

As globally promoted the devil's slogan is to protect the "unborn child" - in science and in the Hebrew Bible - no such thing as "unborn". Jesus was "fruit of thy womb" because He was out of the womb.

The morality that imposes prison terms, economic hardships, contrary to the free will, free choice given to Adam and Eve - even previously given to one-third of the angels in heaven who rebelled against God - has no divine nor godly basis.

It's all devil design using alleged religious men as medium for purposes of window dressing.

God's morality is "love, compassion, kindness, mercy, forgiveness". As the math-chemistry professor in the person of Pope Francis declared: "There is no sin so big that God's love cannot forgive".

With the hourly, daily, global broadcast of the Catholic EWTN tv network promoting the devil's morality, - it is bound to prevail. Combined support consists of 800,000 priests; pastors of over 33,000 non-denominational churches; thousands of Protestant affiliated churches; countless millions of indoctrinated flock - ensure the devil's team as winner.

Be that as it may - the battle for the minds and hearts of humanity continues.

Wickedness in word meanings/application

Millions of zealots that directly, indirectly, or collaterally desire criminalization of miscarriage and/or abortion are clearly not educated or literate to word meanings or applications they have reading or hearing.

In order to address that brutal belief or concept, the most basic/elementary work to do is read, study what the dictionary says and intents to convey. Having said this, the author takes the liberty of referring to the American College Dictionary, prepared by 355 language specialists, published in 1967.

"Page 50. 1. Animal.- Any living thing that is not a plant, generally capable of voluntary motion, sensation, etc. 2. Any animal other than man. 5. Pertaining to the physical, carnal nature of man.

"Page. 392.- Embryo. (Among mammals. . .a young animal during its early stages within the mother's womb); Embryo -organism in its early stage of development; (Posting of Mimi, Yahoo News, 09/3/2019,...If we are talking about developmental stages pre-birth, there is a blastocyst, a zygote, an embryo, or a fetus. I'm guessing basic science is not a big thing in Alabama?)

"Page 447. Fetus, n. Embryol - the young of an animal in the womb;. . .".

"Page 3. Abort v.. t. 1. to miscarry (R.B.J)2. To develop incompletely, remaining in rudimentary state or regeneration. . .

". . .Abortion. The expulsion of human fetus,; page 776. - Miscarriage - premature expulsion of a fetus from the uterus esp. before it is viable. . ."

"5. Person.- a human being whether a man or a woman or a child; a human being distinguished from an animal or a thing..".

N.B. (nota bene). Being .-It means existence as opposed to non-existence. Page 671. Kill. v. t. 1. To deprive (any living creature or thing) of the life in any manner; cause the death; slay. Kill is general word.

In the matter of Roe v. Wade, the most contentious issue on reproductive health in the U.S. since 1973 to current times, HuffPost carried the following story, being quoted on its relevant substantive portion: "In death, Jane Roe finally tells the truth about her life.".

"The Jane Roe of Roe v. Wade, that has become the a mouth piece for the right wing, is ready to tell the world that her decades-old as the shiniest trophy of the anti-abortion movement, was in fact a sham. She took their money - nearly half a million dollars - listened to their explicit coaching, and said what she needed to say.

"But privately, she always believed that if 'a young woman wants to have an abortion. <u>Fine</u>. <u>That's no skin off my ass</u>'. You know that's why they call it choice. It's your choice'. 'So it was all an act?' 'Yeah, says McCorvey, . . . 'I did it well too. I am a good actress. Of course I am not acting now.'". (Confession at her death bed, 2017.)

"Norma McCorvey grew up in a poor family with difficult dynamics. As a young woman she was pregnant three times though she had never an abortion. Her mother cared for her first child Missy, and McCorvey maintained a relationship with Misy until she dies. "... she became a born-again Christian in the mid-1990's, and renounced her sexuality - she was a lesbian - with a long term partner named Connie"

(HuffPost, May 20, 2020.)

Circumventing Roe v. Wade

To by-pass or subjugate the spirit of existing law so more stringent prison terms, restrictions to God-given free will, free choice, which is also protected by the U.S. constitution, the RCC-oriented agenda is pushing for "Life at Conception Act".

U.S. Senator Rand Paul (R-Ky) is one of many proponents. The allegations, recycled many times, as the content of the petition in condensed form as controverting comments being recited as follows.

"Tragically, over 4,000 babies are aborted/(miscarriaged) every day in our nation. Rebut: No such thing as 'baby' inside the uterus - only human embryo/fetus or blastocyst. Miscarriage which results in bleeding requires medical intervention but generally lumped by RCC as fetal/embryonic abortion for its own glorification.

"That's over 1.6 million every year!" Rebut: Typical story telling as long ago claimed by RCC.

Life at Conception Act Petition asserts:

"Because of Roe v. Wade, more than 61 million unborn children have died through abortion". Rebut: No such thing as 'unborn children'. The human embryo/fetus/blastocyst - even with heartbeat - (as almost all mammals at that stage) - does not become human being in law, in the Bible because God does not invest the soul/spirit into that living thing. A recycled claim of the agenda-initiator, the RCC.

"The 14th Amendment . . .states: 'nor shall any state deprive any person of life, liberty or property. . .". Rebut: In the Ark of the Covenant given to Moses, the ordinance 'thou shall not kill' (murder as explained by many rabbis) addressed as relationship to discerning human beings among humans.

Author commented on Facebook on Nov. 18, 2020 as follows:

"The ferocious global work of RCC against abortion has some similarity to wiping heretics in the 12th century to 18th century. The RCC interlocked, interwoven into Catholic-dominated empires for centuries perpetrated torture, murder of young, old, infirmed humans in imposing its cruel agenda.

"In current times the similarity is the use of State power imposing prison terms in effecting its fallacious, anti-Christ, anti-science iron hand in ending abortion. For centuries - the same doctrine of the evil means justify the end.

"Brief argument on the lies of RCC: The fetus/embryo/living organ/living thing by science, by God-Jesus, by the Holy Bible, in all aspects because it is not human being - no soul, no soul whatever. God is love, merciful, forgiving would never support man-made prison terms. . . Prison terms would thwart the God-given right of Free will, free Choice, human freedom. The only mention in the Holy Bible about accidental miscarriage and abortion is when there is fight or struggle that the perpetrator becomes liable for civil damages. . .".

In the Yahoo News headline "Leader of US Catholic bishops: Biden's stances pose dilemma", the author commented: ' . . . miscarriage and abortion essentially the same that requires medical intervention; that the fetus/embryo is organ in the woman's body; . . God exercises final judgment and penalty when the mortal/physical being is dead as dead, and the soul/spirit faces the unseen, invisible God.'".

Commentary on Nov. 22, 2020.

2/Circumventing Roe v. Wade

"Science is clear that human life begins at conception when a new human being is formed;' and . . . ." Rebut: False; a deception. A precise definition of human being is given by over 100 authors in the American College Dictionary. A human embryo/fetus/is not human being; the word 'human' being used to distinguish it from that of the animal.

"The American people oppose abortion-on-demand and want innocent human life to be protected . . . .; Rebut: No human being inside the womb; the intention and goal of the RCC agenda is its own self-serving gratification by using the strong arm of the government in imposing prison terms and for civil society to imprint shame, defamation on those who exercise the God-given right as well as the libertarian right of free will and free choice; more over impose severe financial difficulties on the woman's own body.

The RCC-initiated agenda of lies, omissions, deception finds support among many pastors who cite among others biblical passages. They cite King David, Jeremiah, Joseph said to had been told "I know you before you were born; . . . that you were born for a purpose . . ." Rebut: The flaws to this argument, among others are: The application being specific, particular to these prophets at the biblical time and place; what the Lord God chooses regardless of time, place, situations, circumstances, can prevent, overrule any attempt of miscarriage or abortion; that it is pure illogical that the purpose for each human being must apply to the billions already born and yet to be born.

rgb.

Calls For Prison Terms

Powerful politicians blinded or misguided by the global initiatives, relentless push on by almost 800,000 RC priests, millions of accomplices, the drive for prison terms who exercise free will, free choice on miscarriage and/or abortion continues to be bolder and bigger.

To build more support for the demonic RCC agenda, there is in the US Congress the Republican idea of skipping the law on Roe v. Wade. So as not to frontally overturn this law, the prison-term zealots are demanding for lawmakers to pass "a Life at Conception Act" to end abortion (and miscarriage too).

Attendant to that forceful prison-term movement, the alleged Pro-Life/Anti-abortion group issued the multi-purpose Citizen Petition to Overturn Roe v. Wade to millions of mailing recipients. The petition cited eight allegations/ assertions starting with "Whereas" worded as if they are gospel truths. Five of the "whereas" cited in gist below.

". . . Because of Roe v. Wade, more than 62 million unborn children have died through abortion, and ". . . Roe v. Wade, the SCOTUS declared it could not resolve the difficult question of when life begins; ". . . The 14th Amendment . . . states: "nor shall the state deprive any person of life, liberty or property . . . nor deny any person . . .equal protection of the law;

". . . In Roe, the Supreme Court admitted: 'If . . . personhood (of unborn) is established, the appellant's case . . . collapses, for the fetus' right is guaranteed . . .;
". . . Science is clear that human life begins at conception, when a new human being is formed;..."

The mailings produce millions of revenue; the uninformed, the educated derelicts, the myopic intellectuals, the do-nothings become contributors to the falsehoods, omissions, deceptions.

While prosecutors in general are bound to prosecute violators of the law, in the specific law on miscarriage/abortion, many are hesitant or with reservations in carrying out this role.

To prosecutors, the criminal aspect of abortion/miscarriage law is rather awkward as it involves the person's right or exercise of reproductive health. (In fine - it hurts nobody - but some ego.)

"Dozens of state and local prosecutors released a statement vowing not to enforce extreme anti-restrictions passed in their states.

"As elected prosecutors with charging discretion, we choose not to prosecute individuals pursuant to these deepl concerning laws" - issued by Fair and Just Prosecution - an advocacy group.

"The statement is signed by 42 elected officials including 12 state attorneys general. The signers represent jurisdictions in 24 states including Georgia, Alabama, Texas and Ohio, which are among those that have recently passed or proposed laws sharply restricting or outright banning abortion (miscarriage).

"To fulfill our obligations as prosecutors and ministers of justice, to preserve the integrity of the system, and keep our communities safe and healthy it is imperative that we use our discretion. . .".

(Quotes from "Over 40 Prosecutors Refuse to Enforce New Anti-Abortion Laws" - HuffPost, June 7, 2019)
1252021

As recapitulation/summary of the lies, omissions, deception, wickedness of anti-abortionists and/or pro-life warriors

*   Fetus/embryo is never a human being because it has no soul which Almighted God does not invest
*   Fetus/embryo is part of the woman's organ in the developing stage
*   It is not a person nor human being both in science and in the Holy Bible
*   It is not being killed or murdered because it is not a human being with a soul
*   Before the stage of being fetus, it is a blastocyst, a zygote
*   While still in the uterus/womb, it remains a zygote, blastocyst or fetus, not a child
*   A born child becomes a person if it survives outside the womb on its own on the fifth day and God breath into it the breath of life called soul

* God made Adam and Eve with free will, free choice - God even gave the legion of Lucifer freewill to be for Him or be against Him
* Man-made morality is man-made
* Man-made passion, self-centeredness, rigidity is for his own benefit

Bonus Page - About God Bible Science Creation/2021

Miscarriage, abortion, LGBTQ - all about physical, mundane and spiritual realm - settles down to God - His existence, power, - all works of creation.

Here is what many research scientists studied, analyzed, evaluated, discussed, and arrived at.

"Dr. Ariel Roth (over 33 years research) examines the key issues related to the 'God Question'".
"The intricate organization of matter in the universe; the precision of the forces in physics; the complexity of the eye and the brain; the elaborate genetic code; the disparity between the fossil record and the vast amount of time necessary for evolution".

His book: Origins Linking Science and Scriptures which presents scientific evidence that authenticates the Bible has been published in 17 languages. A new book titled Science Discovers God: Seven Convincing Lines of Evidence for His Existence. Available in (Seventh) Adventist Book Center.

Dr. Roth's affirmations are supported by books of other scientists, among whom are:

Origin by Design - Robert H Brown, et al.; Understanding Creation - Humberto Rasi; Incredible Creatures That Defy Evolution - Dr. Jobe Martin.

Based on his academic, work, and experience background being way past 75, writer wrote in social media - written and digital - as fact that LGBTQ, gender orientation, invisible thoughts, spirit/soul, mixing of genes, brain cells, DNA, sensory organs - and whatever - is not man-made but God-made.

The Case Against the Punishers, Initiators, lawmakers

There are over 500,000 priests, nuns, deacons, lay ministers who insists on the man-made agenda against women who exercise free will/ free choice on the autonomy of their body.

The fallacy of that cruel, ungodly agenda consist of the following:

1. The miscarriage/expulsion of the union of sperm and egg cell is not "killing' within the meaning of 'Thou shalt not kill' ordinance. The facts are: The 'thing "it" is not a human being with a soul/spirit; the claim of heartbeat does not qualify as human being because the fetus/ embryos of animals have been known to veterinarians as having heartbeats; Jewish rabbis learned in the Holy Bible are of the consensus that the fetus/fertilized egg to be deemed lived human being God must first breathe the life-giving soul on its way out of the uterus; that the word n killing 11 is actually murder, i.e., done with malice, evil purpose and being addressed in God's ordinance to human beings with soul, with

discernment of right and wrong; God requires the "being" to have a soul/ spirit so when the physical body dies, the soul/ spirit becomes accountable of what its life has been when it comes to God's judgment of compassion, mercy, forgiveness or condemnation. No soul, nothing.

2. Above all since the first humans- Adam and Eve were created by the Being of light- free will, free choice was given to them. Without free will, it was impossible for the serpent of tempting them into eating the fruit of knowledge, as there was an abundance of other fruits. Free will, free choice God validated them - as then, later, in current times. God has not rescinded, cancelled, nor withdrawn that free gift He endowed all humans, particularly women over the dignity, temple of HIS likeness, autonomy of the female body.

3. The "morality n the punishers, initiators, lawmakers imposing on women with fear of sever punishment- given a deeper, behind-the- scene application really discloses itself as the morality version of the devil. Why? Simple. Because their agenda has no kindness, no compassion, no mercy, no forgiveness. Just prison, prison, retribution for disobedience to their agenda.

Why Abortion Should Remain Legal (and liberalized)

The RCC- the greatest global power against abortion - and its control over the greatest portion of humanity is at error/ incorrect/ in falsehood. The grounds are:

1. The entity did not, cannot prove in biblical and mundane terms the union of the sperms and egg cell more known as fetus in the womb is human being endowed by God with soul or spirit accountable to Him in the afterlife ;

2. It cannot prove the fetus has free will, with discernment as required at the time of God's Judgment ;

3. That in fact the global attack on abortion is a cultural/ political/ tradition thing for image-building purposes that the institution is "righteous" or holder of the.. truths.. on Christianization/ or its claim of "infallibility";

4. That it could not prove nor show cause or causes why abortionists and medical providers with certainty having their souls go to hell;

5. On the contrary the religious corporation has been, is and remains publicly known for centuries for lies, omissions, deceptions, hijackings, consisting of, among many such as: St. Peter is founder of its church, alternately Jesus is founder of its church and religion - in fact both raised, lived, preached and crucified as Hebrew Jews; it is the protector, champion, pursuer of human life but in fact for over 500 years the institution murdered millions in the various Crusades, Conquesta, religious wars, "Christianization" and rule and colonization of the world ;

6. Its political, cultural, social, religious, economic history as it was then to current times cannot be trusted nor honored with honesty, truth, and credibility.

In view of the foregoing statement of facts, it is the better judgment that U.S. lawmakers stay out of the abortion debate. They ought to rescind the severe penalties of incarceration they imposed on abortion and to the medical providers. The man-made punishments being imposed have "no legs to stand on" .. -biblically, morally, rationally.

True Stories on the After Life

Source: WAKING UP IN HEAVEN -A true Story of Brokennes, Heaven and Life Again - Crystal McVea and Alex Tresnioiski, 2016, 216 pages, Howard Books, 1230

Avenue of the Americas, New York, NY 10020.

"I live in a small town in Southern Oklahoma, in a community of friendly and God- fearing people. . .

"While seriously ill in the hospital she died; her soul at an instant left her body and instantly was in heaven. Absolute peace, beauty beyond any earthly image, meeting relatives and friends who were long gone. When soul/spirit returned to body after nine minutes, God gave her this message: "Tell them what you can remember"

"I struggled I'm the least likely person to tell anyone about God.... Early in my life I was a sinner, and I am pretty sure I broke everyone in the Ten Commandments. That's right - not just some - all the ten. Even the big one -Thou Shalt Not Kill"

"In heaven there is no time- minutes or seconds- everything happens all at the same time."

"In spite of all the mistakes, mischiefs, frailties, bad, ungodly things in her life the wisdom she learned on the short moment in heaven- she learned thru the trials and challenges that God loved, cared for her and reciprocated God's love her own love for Him." God is always love- no anger, no retribution, no getting even, no vengeance.

SOURCE: DYING TO WAKE UP- A Doctor's Voyage into the Afterlife and the Wisdom He Brought Back Rajiv Parti, M.D. and Paul Perry, SimondSchuster.com, 2016, Atria Books

His story is about how he- being a Hindu met the invisible, unseen God while his physical body was in the emergency room, his soul departed to the bright tunnel. His soul/ spirit was in this place where there was absolute peace, joy, where the surroundings so bright, beautiful nothing comparable to anything earthly or mundane.

The soul was guided by some angels where he met deceased family members. His family's life of opulence, gated community, fancy cars, dwelling in a mansion, lifestyle of comfort and abundance kept f lashing back to him. All things happening at the same time the soul being was given some unpleasant messages of the kind of person he was to his fellow humans.

That he was self-centered to the life of comfort, abundance, but uncaring for fellow humans, lacking empathy to others who are in need. The many conversations carried on by the Being of light (that is, God) with the soul not by mouth but something like mind-to-mind, brain-to-brain.

Directly and indirectly the feelings of joy, peace, beyond earthly perception were projections of God's love, kindness, compassion. In his own words:

"The voice came into my mind again." We are all born naked and the same. It is later we acquire pride and prejudice ... And anger and addiction and ego and fears, I thought to my telepathic friend (Being of Light). What happened to me? Why I have become so self-centered? Why do I care more for things than people?"

Love, compassion, kindness, care for others - constitutes the Wisdom that bugged him after the soul joined the physical body. So he gave up the lucrative practice of anesthesiology and to current times he practices "Consciousness Healing" to help those who are experiencing different types of pains. He gives lectures throughout the US to share his experiences of healing.

Sources/ Bibliography/ Reference

The Holy Bible, -authorized King James Version, World Bible Publishers, Iowa Falls, Iowa Printed in England Her Majesty's Printers

Holy Bible, Heirloom Bible Publishers, / DeVore & Sons Inc, 1988, Wichita, Kansas

What the Gospels Meant - Garry Wills Vking Press, 2008, 375 Hudson St., New York, NY

The American College Dictionary, C.L. Barnhart, Editor in Chief, 1967, Random House, New York

To Heaven and Back by Mary C. Neal, MD, 2017, Water Brook Press, 12265 Oracle Blvd., Suite 200, Colorado Springs. CO 80921

God and the After Life by Jeffrey: Long MD and Paul Perry, 2016, Harper-Collins Publishers, 195 Broadway, New York, NY 10007

Ancient Secrets of the Bible, published by American Bible Society, 2012, P O Box 11016, Des Moines, IA 50336-1016

Dying to Wake Up by Rajiv Parti MD and Paul Perry, 2016, Simon & Schuster/ Atria Books New York London

America Needs Fatima, solicitation, Feb., 2012, Hanover, Pennsylvania

EWTN Global Network - 24/7, Irondale, Alabama and solicitation, 2014

Missionary Oblates, solicitation, Belleville, Illinois 8/22/ 2014

Association of Marian Helpers, solicitation, Stockbridge, Mass 01263

Salesian Missions. Solicitation, New Rochelle, New York 10802

Freemasonry & Its Repercussions by Ross Brillantes, Outskirts Press, 2013, Parker, CO

Conqueror-Empires / Agenda/ Purposes of the Five Empires by Ross Brillantes, May 2017, DiggyPod Press, Austin, Texas

Printed in the United States
by Baker & Taylor Publisher Services